GREAT PEOPLE

MARCO POLO

The World Traveller

Gerry Bailey and Karen Foster
Illustrated by Leighton Noyes
and Karen Radford

hachette
INDIA

DIGBY is a treasure collector. Every Saturday he picks up a bargain at Mr Rummage's bric-a-brac stall and loves listening to the story behind his new 'find'.

HESTER is Digby's argumentative nine-year-old sister – and she doesn't believe a word that Mr Rummage says!

Mr RUMMAGE has a stall piled high with many curious objects – and he has a great story to tell about each and every one.

KENZO the barber has a wig or hairpiece for every dressing-up occasion, and is always happy to put his scissors to use!

Mrs BILGE pushes her dustcart around the marketplace, picking up litter. Trouble is, she's always throwing away the objects on Mr Rummage's stall...

Mr CLUMPMUGGER has an amazing collection of ancient maps, dusty books and old newspapers in his Rare Prints kiosk.

CHRISSY's Genuine Vintage Clothing stand has all the costumes Digby and Hester need to act out the characters in Mr Rummage's stories.

YOUSSEF has travelled far and wide and carries a bag full of souvenirs from his exciting journeys.

SAFFRON sells pots and pans, herbs, spices, oils, soaps and dyes from her exotic Spice Kitchen rigged up under a shady awning.

BUZZ is a street vendor with all the gossip. He sells sweets and pastries from a tray that's strapped to his back.

COLONEL KARBUNCLE sells military uniforms, medals, flags, swords, helmets, cannon balls, gas masks – all from the boot of his battered jeep.

PIXIE the fortune-teller sells incense, lotions and potions, candles, mandalas and crystals inside her exotic New Age tent.

PRU is a dreamer and Hester's best friend. She likes to tag along, especially when make-up and dressing up is involved.

JAKE is Digby's chum. He's got a lively imagination and is always up to mischief.

MR POLLOCK's toyshop is crammed with string puppets, rocking horses, model planes, wooden animals – and he makes them all himself!

Every Saturday morning, Knick-Knack Market comes to life. The street traders are there almost before the sun is up. And by the time you and I have got out of bed, the stalls are built, the boxes opened and all the goods carefully laid out on show.

Objects are piled high. Some are laid out on velvet: precious brooches and jewelled swords. Others stand upright at the back: large, framed pictures of very important people, lamps made from tasselled satin, and old-fashioned washstands – the sort that drip when you pour the water in. And then there are things that stay in their boxes all day, waiting for the right customer to come along: war medals laid out in straight lines, stopwatches on chains, and cutlery in polished silver for all those special occasions.

But Rummage's stall is different. Rummage of Knick-Knack Market has a stall piled high with a higgledy-piggledy jumble of things that no-one could ever want. For who'd want to buy a stuffed mouse? Or a broken penknife? Or a pair of false teeth?

Well, Rummage has them all. And, as you can imagine, they don't cost a lot!

Digby Platt – seven-year-old collector of antiques – was off to see his friend, Mr Rummage of Knick-Knack Market. It was Saturday and, as usual, Digby's weekly allowance was burning a hole in his pocket.

But Digby wasn't going to spend it on any old thing. It had to be something rare and interesting for his collection, something from Mr Rummage's incredible stall. Hester, his older sister, had come along, too. She had secret doubts about the value of Mr Rummage's objects and felt, for some big-sisterly reason, that she had to stop her little brother from buying 'useless bits of junk'.

'Hello, Mr Rummage, hi, Youssef,' said Digby cheerfully.

'Hello, there,' replied Youssef, then he turned back to Rummage, 'Twelve pounds, Mr Rummage, and that's a good offer.'

'Let's say eight pounds... Hi, kids,' said Rummage.

'Eleven pounds,' said Youssef.

'Ten pounds…'

'Oh, all right then, it's yours for ten pounds,' said Youssef. 'You drive a hard bargain, my friend.'

'What was that all about?' asked Digby.

'They're haggling, numbskull – trying to agree on a price for whatever *that* is,' said Hester.

'It's a silk purse,' said Rummage.

'Looks a bit tatty to me,' said Hester dryly.

'That's because it's old,' said Youssef. 'It once belonged to a very famous traveller and explorer.'

'Marco Polo, to be exact,' said Rummage, digging around inside the purse, 'and let me see… there's a piece of paper. Hmm, old Chinese paper money. Looks like a Yuan note.'

'A what note?' said Digby.

'The Chinese called their money Yuan,' said Rummage. 'In fact, they were the first people to use paper money, which is why Marco Polo brought it back from his travels.'

'So how many Yuan is the note worth – a thousand maybe?'

'This one's just ten Yuan,' said Rummage.

'So it's not worth much then,' grumbled Digby, sounding disappointed.

'Not in Yuan, but it's actually worth a lot nowadays, because it's so old,' said Rummage smiling.

 # Marco Polo

Marco Polo was probably born in Venice, Italy, in 1254 – although some say he was born in Korcula in Yugoslavia and moved to Venice with his family when he was a boy. His father, Nicolo Polo, was a merchant, but we don't know who his mother was.

Marco Polo was one of the first Europeans to visit China, and his journey inspired other explorers for years to come. Using his records, map-makers were able to draw up new charts that included the eastern lands he visited – lands no-one had heard of before. His book, called *The Travels*, is one of the most famous travel diaries ever written.

But let's find out more...

Venice was a great trading city when Marco Polo was a young lad. Exotic goods from the East, such as precious jewels, perfumes, silks and spices, strange animals and rare foodstuffs were brought here by ship, then traded throughout Europe. Venetian merchants had become rich and powerful. Venice was also a centre of the arts, and hundreds of artists and craftsmen laboured in its studios and workshops. Marco would have soaked up all of this, along with the beauty and pageantry of the city.

Marco's dream

Like many other boys in 13th century Venice, Marco probably played in the dockyards. He would have enjoyed listening to sailors' stories about the wonderful things they'd seen – distant lands, strange peoples and fabulous treasures just waiting to be discovered. He probably dreamed of becoming a merchant and sailing to far-off places himself. After all, he was a clever, adventurous boy living in an exciting town during an interesting period in history.

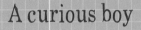

A curious boy

We don't know exactly what kind of education Marco received. But he probably learned all the basic stuff that boys from good families learned at the time – arithmetic, reading and perhaps philosophy. However, we do know that Marco was good at languages and learned to speak at least four. He was intelligent, quick-witted and had a brilliant mind for detail. He was also interested in people and other ways of life, so he must have had a rich imagination.

'Marco Polo lived in the fabulous city of Venice,' Rummage continued. 'an important port and rich trading centre on the east coast of what is now Italy. Like many boys of his age, he probably went down to the docks every day to watch the ships come and go with their cargos of silks, spices and other rich and exotic treasures.'

'Did Marco want to be a merchant or a sailor, then?' asked Digby.

'He probably wanted to be both, but merchants made more money than sailors,' said Youssef.

'Marco's mother died when he was very young, so he was brought up by an aunt and uncle,' said Rummage. 'They taught him everything he needed to know to become a merchant – how to use foreign money, what goods would trade well and make a profit, and how to run a merchant ship.'

'Wow! I'd like to do that,' exclaimed Digby. 'I'd travel the world and visit strange lands so I could pick up all sorts of interesting bargains to bring back and sell to Mr Rummage.'

'That'd make a change,' sighed Hester. 'But before you go anywhere, why don't you start by selling off some of the weird stuff that's cluttering up your bedroom?'

'What happened to Marco's father?' asked Digby.

'Well, Nicolo Polo had already made a journey to Cathay, as China was called by the Europeans in those days,' said Youssef. 'The trip had taken 15 years, so Marco wouldn't even have known whether he was alive or not.'

'It must've been a surprise when he finally turned up,' said Hester.

'It was,' said Rummage. 'When Nicolo returned to Venice with his brother Maffeo, who'd gone with him on the trip, it must have been a dream come true for Marco.'

'Just imagine!' said Youssef. 'Nicolo would've arrived on the doorstep and said, "Hi Marco, I'm back – and I've brought you lots of interesting things from some really amazing places..." Then he would've told him all about where he'd been and the people he'd met, especially the Great Khan.'

'Who was the Great Khan?' asked Digby.

'Kublai Khan was the emperor of the Mongol world. The Mongols had come from the plains of Central Asia. They'd conquered most of Asia and China by the time Nicolo got there, and Kublai was now their king and

emperor,' said Youssef.

'I wonder what sort of presents they brought back for Marco,' said Hester.

'They probably brought things like exotic clothes, satin slippers, pictures printed on rice paper, and maybe even a silkworm or two,' said Rummage.

'You mean worms made from silk?' asked Digby.

'No, I mean worms that spin silk, Digby. Incredible, isn't it? Uptil then, Europeans thought silk came from a plant! Anyway, Marco was so enthralled by all the stories that he begged his father to take him along when he and his uncle Maffeo next returned to China.'

Nicolo and Maffeo's adventure 1254-1269

A trading trip

In 1254, Nicolo and Maffeo Polo left Venice for Constantinople, now the Turkish city of Istanbul. They were searching for new markets and wares, and bought and sold goods along the way. Eventually, they moved on to Russia and then decided to head back. But they found their route home blocked because a tribal war had broken out, so they travelled south-east to the bustling town of Bukhara in Uzbekistan. Here, they spent three years trading in furs, salt, wood, and slaves. They were also lucky enough to meet the ambassador to the great Mongol emperor Kublai Khan, who invited them to travel with him all the way to China. Nicolo and Maffeo jumped at the chance.

KUBLAI KHAN

KUBLAI KHAN RULED A HUGE EMPIRE THAT STRETCHED FROM THE YELLOW SEA IN THE EAST TO THE BLACK SEA IN THE WEST

 ## Peking, China

When the Polos arrived in Peking, Kublai Khan treated them as honoured guests. In fact, he came to trust them more than he trusted his conquered Chinese subjects, and wanted to find out as much as he could about their homeland. When they presented him with letters of greeting from the Pope in Rome, Kublai politely asked them to pay his respects to the Pope when they returned and to come back with 100 priests and some holy oil. He said he wanted to learn more about Christianity. When it was time to go, Kublai gave the Polos a golden tablet – a kind of passport granting them three years' free lodging and food and guides for the return journey.

'How do we know the Polos' stories are true?' asked Hester, who often found it hard to believe everything Rummage told them.

'Luckily, Marco took notes so he wouldn't forget the strange and wonderful things he'd seen,' said Youssef. 'Later on, he described his travels to a man called Rustichello of Pisa, who wrote them down in a famous book that everyone wanted to read – a sort of diary.'

'Huh, diaries are so boring,' said Hester. 'I bet Marco exaggerated his stories just to make them more interesting.'

'He probably didn't need to,' said Rummage. 'The lands he described were fantastic enough to people who knew nothing of Asia. But Marco didn't always write down what he saw himself, sometimes he recorded what other travellers told him, including the odd myth and tall tale, probably because he was a bit superstitious.'

The Polos' caravan

Marco set off with his father and uncle in 1271. He was just 17 years old. First, they stopped off at Rome to find the 100 friars Kublai Khan had asked for. But the Pope could only spare two! From Rome they sailed for Acre, now the Israeli port of Haifa. There they stopped off to pick up the bottle of holy oil from the Church of the Holy Sepulchre that Nicolo had promised to the Khan. Marco was a lively travelling companion. Everyone was impressed with how he could remember things and by the way he picked up foreign languages so quickly.

Bloodthirsty bandits!

The journey was hazardous from the start. From Acre, the Polos trekked south across rough and lonely roads, where bloodthirsty bandits lay in wait around every corner. Tribal warfare and plagues meant the travellers were in constant danger. Soon, everything became too much to bear for the cowardly friars and they turned back, leaving the Polos on their own.

THE POLOS TRAVELLED IN A CARAVAN OF MERCHANTS AND PACK ANIMALS, FOR SAFETY AND COMPANIONSHIP

Wild winds

In his diary, Marco wrote of the scorching hot winds that blew across the land. They were so fierce, he said, that anyone trying to cross the desert when they blew, would have the moisture drained from their bodies until their skin burned and crumbled into dust. The Polos had to sit in water up to their necks to protect themselves from the heat while they waited for the wind to die down so they could continue their journey.

Dhow death traps

The Polos crossed the dry and dusty plains of Armenia and made their way into Persia – which Marco describes as a land of dates and parrots. Thinking they could save time by sailing from the Persian Gulf to China, they went down to the Hormuz harbour to look for a boat. But one look at the 'dhows' moored there changed their minds. Held together with coconut string and wooden pegs, Marco said they were death traps. Now the Polos had to turn back and head for Cathay overland.

'The Polos, like so many travellers before them, followed the old Silk Road to get to their final destination in Cathay,' said Rummage.

'A road made of silk!' exclaimed Digby. 'How could that…'

'It wasn't really made of silk, Digby' interrupted Youssef. 'It got the name because the merchants who used it brought silk back from Cathay.'

'What a dingbat,' giggled Hester. 'A road made of silk…'

'So how long was this road?' asked Digby, ignoring his sister.

'It was very, very long. And, in spite of its name, it wasn't just one road but a series of trails and mountain passes that stretched from China to the eastern shores of the Mediterranean. Some went further north, almost into Russia, while others turned south into India and Arabia.'

Treasures from the East

Merchants risked their lives to travel the Silk Road because the rewards were high. The exotic items they brought back from China and elsewhere sold for high prices in their own countries, while the gold, silver and other materials they took with them fetched a good price in the East. Over the Silk Road to the West came nutmeg, cinnamon and cloves from India, perfumes from Arabia, rubies and lapis lazuli from Afghanistan, pearls from Baghdad, turquoise from Turkey and silk and brocade from China.

Along the Silk Road

Palaces and pavilions

For over 3,000 years the great Silk Road was the longest land route in the world. It originally connected the Roman Empire to China and stretched for more than 12,850 kilometres, linking regions as different as Russia, Africa, Arabia, India and Persia. Marco would have gazed open-mouthed at the golden spires and jewelled domes of palaces and pavilions as the Polos' caravan wound through the hills and valleys. For the road was lined with splendid cities whose romantic names are still recognized today – Samarkand, Baghdad, Jeddah and Karakorum.

THE BLUE MOSQUE,
ISTANBUL, TURKEY

THE TILLA-KARI MOSQUE,
SAMARKAND, UZBEKISTAN

 # From Persia to the Hindu Kush

Bitter water

From Hormuz, the Polos travelled north-east to Kerman and then across an 'empty desert full of poisonous water as green as grass'. In fact, the water was probably just unusually salty and undrinkable. They made their way to Mashdad (now Meshed, Timochain) and then followed the north Persian border to the east where an excited Marco heard the tribal story of Aloeddin's band of assassins.

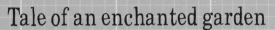

Tale of an enchanted garden

An old man named Aloeddin lived in a castle overlooking a beautiful valley. There he grew a scented garden, filling it with exotic flowers, fruit trees, and streams running with wine and honey. He entertained his warriors there, letting them eat and drink their fill until they agreed to carry out his orders. The warriors were so enchanted by the wonders of the garden, they were prepared to kill all of Aloeddin's enemies so they could live in there for ever. Aloeddin's band of assassins rampaged the land until Aloeddin's castle was destroyed by the Great Khan's Mongol armies.

Valley of horses

At last the Polos reached the shadows of the mighty Hindu Kush mountains. Marco tells us that the plains of Balashan were overrun by a herd of magnificient wild horses bred from Alexander the Great's famous steed, Bucephalus! The Polos liked the place so much, they decided to spend a year there, so Marco could recover from an illness and enjoy the fresh mountain air.

'Sometimes the Polos journeyed with just their own small caravan, but then they'd join bigger caravans that were going in the same direction,' Rummage went on.

'How come they had caravans, when they didn't have cars?' wondered Digby.

'Here we go again,' said Hester. 'Not caravans on wheels, silly.'

Rummage laughed, 'No, indeed. A caravan is another name for a group of merchants who travel together for safety, as well as companionship. Merchants like the Polos would hire camels or assess to carry their goods, and sometimes they hired guides to show them the way.'

'The Polos must have seen some wonderful things,' said Hester.

'They did,' said Pixie the fortune-teller, who'd left her New Age Tent to join them. 'They would have seen glittering salt mountains and rainbow-coloured hills, and once they even found gemstones like jasper and quartz lying in a river bed.'

'How did they get there?' asked Digby, boggle-eyed.

'They must have been washed down from the Himalayas by mountain streams,' she said.

'Marco also tells of another region called Balashan where rubies were mined from the mountains,' added Rummage. 'Only the king was allowed to dig them up, though. Because there were so many gems, he needed to keep their price high.'

'A clever king,' said Pixie.

19

'Marco also wrote about the wildlife he saw on his travels – strange-looking cows with shaggy coats and straggly beards, called yaks, and woolly sheep with huge, curly horns,' Youssef went on.

'What about hawks and falcons? Weren't they used for hunting once?' asked Digby.

'They certainly were. In fact, the falcons Marco saw were so large and fierce they could even pick up a lamb in their talons and fly off with it.'

'And what about camels?' said Hester.

'What about them, Miss Humpty Hester?' giggled Digby.

'Keep quiet,' replied his sister, sternly.

'Now, now children,' interrupted Rummage. 'I was about to say that the Polos probably crossed the desert on camels, so they wouldn't need to keep stopping at waterholes on the way.'

'That's because camels store their food and water in their humps, isn't it, Mr Rummage?'

'Yes, Digby. Anyway, in a place called Bargu, Marco saw strange "bargelak" birds, with a swallow's forked tail and claws like a parrot. Close by he also saw "gudderi," a kind of antelope that the people got musk from.'

'What's musk' asked Hester.

'It's an animal oil used to make perfume. I've got some in my tent if you want to try it,' said Pixie.

'Yuk!' exclaimed Hester, wrinkling her nose. 'I don't think so!'

On top of the world

On the cliff edge

After his rest, Marco and the band of travellers headed north-east through Vokhan, which we now call the Wakkan Valley. It was a steep and gruelling climb. The pack animals jostled to get a foothold on the stony ground, and the mountain air was filled with the sound of the bleating of sheep, bells jangling noisily around their necks. The caravan moved slowly on, winding around hairpin bends and trailing along the edge of sheer cliffs that dropped away to ravines far below.

Peaks and pinnacles

Three days later, they reached the green foothills of the fabulous Pamir mountain range, where they scaled peak after peak. Marco wrote it was like being at the top of the world – so high, in fact, that no bird could fly that high. He also complained they couldn't cook food properly because their campfire burned less brightly up there where the air was so thin.

Singing sands

At last, the Polos reached the plains of Kashcar. But they weren't over the worst yet. When the caravan reached the Tamir Basin, they were forced to cross a vast desert. Marco believed it was home to evil spirits who drove travellers to their deaths. He'd heard stories of merchants who'd lagged behind their caravan and heard the spirits calling to them, luring them deeper into the desert to die. It was said that bands of ghost warriors might gallop towards them across the shimmering sands, causing them to flee and lose their way. So the Polos decided to camp in a circle and put bells around their animals at night to stop them from straying. Of course, now we know these spirits are nothing other than mirages brought on by the blistering heat of the desert.

'After crossing the Pamir mountains, the Polos made good progress until they reached the edge of the Gobi Desert. At its narrowest point, it took 40 days to cross, and waterholes were at least a day's journey apart. They would've had to carry their own water to survive,' said Rummage.

'So did they try to cross it?' asked Digby.

'No, they skirted around it. But the Polos' guides would've known what a bleak place it was. It still is today – although Mongol herders, the ones who live in round tents called "yurts," still make it their home.'

'I wouldn't want to live there,' stated Hester.

'Then you'd have loved the place Marco arrived at three years after leaving home – the magnificent summer palace of Kublai Khan. The Chinese called it Shang-tu, but we probably know it better as Xanadu,' said Youssef.

'Xanadu,' said Hester, dreamily. 'Mmm, sounds really exotic.'

The White Feast

The White Feast, was the most important celebration of the year. Everyone wore white as it was considered lucky. On that day the Great Khan would drink 'kumiss', the milk from his royal herd of white mares. Whenever he lifted his cup, musicians would begin to play and everyone had to kneel down until he'd finished his drink. And they had to do it every time – or else! At the end of the day, he received gifts of gold, silver, precious stones, beautiful milk-white horses and a lot of dazzling white robes. In return, Kublai gave lands to the nobles whose presents he liked best!

Xanadu

Marco Polo was very impressed by the great banquets Kublai Khan and his court enjoyed at Xanadu. The banqueting hall, he said, held 6,000 people who would feast for days while jugglers and acrobats entertained them. Astrologers and magicians also attended, and cast spells to make flagons fill up with wine and move through the air to the Khan's table! Servants carrying food and drink had to cover their faces with silken veils so they didn't breathe on what they were serving!

ON FEAST DAYS, THE KHAN WOULD ORDER HIS 5,000 ELEPHANTS TO PARADE BEFORE HIM: IMAGINE, IF EACH ONE TOOK FIVE SECONDS TO PASS, THE WHOLE PARADE WOULD TAKE SEVEN HOURS AND THERE WOULD BE A LOT OF CLEANING UP TO DO!

The summer palace

The Khan's marble and gold summer palace at Xanadu was surrounded by walls 25 km long that enclosed gardens and lakes. Inside the walls, thousands of birds and animals roamed free, while groves of incense trees gave off the sweet smell of cedar and jasmine.

The royal pavilion

In the middle of the garden, the Great Khan had built a pavilion supported by a colonnade of gold and varnished pillars. Around each one a dragon entwined its tail, while its head held up the roof. A bamboo shelter kept out the rain. The building was supported on each side by 200 very strong silken cords that secured it to the ground, like a tent. It was so well built, that it could be taken down and put up again in no time.

'Did Marco learn to speak Chinese?' asked Digby.

'No, he didn't,' replied Rummage. 'But he spoke the Mongol language, which was more useful. Don't forget, the Mongols were in charge. They ruled China after conquering it.'

'Didn't the Chinese hate that, though,' said Hester.

'They weren't happy, obviously. Kublai ruled them fairly but very firmly. And because they were rebellious, he never really trusted them – which is why he preferred to have foreigners act as his advisers.'

'So if Marco had been Chinese, he wouldn't have got the job,' said Hester.

'That's right.' said Rummage.

'What job?' asked Digby. 'Was he a falconer? That's what I'd have been.'

'No, Marco became one of Kublai's ambassadors,' said Rummage. 'He spent 17 years in the East, travelling far and wide across the Khan's lands. Marco knew how fascinated Kublai was by the customs of his people, so he carefully noted everything he saw and heard. Later on, he put the

most interesting stories in his travel book. Of course, he also added a lot of the tales he'd heard from other travellers, too.'

Peking

KUBLAI KHAN PLANTED THE GARDENS OF HIS PALACE IN PEKING WITH FAVOURITE TREES FROM ALL OVER HIS EMPIRE

Marco never forgot his first glimpse of Peking (now Beijing), which the Mongols called Kanbalu. Set above the city was the Great Khan's palace, richly decorated with golden dragons and paintings of birds, animals and battle scenes. Marco says that the roof shone in the sunshine with a dazzling array of bright colours. And inside the palace grounds stood a green mountain surrounded by a silver lake teeming with exotic fish. Each day, the Great Khan would go to the magnificent pavilion perched at the top to 'refresh his spirit'.

Royal baths

Marco was fascinated by the Chinese method of heating their baths. He noted they used 'black stones that burn like logs' to keep fires burning from morning to evening. The Chinese needed the fuel (which we now know to be coal) because it was their habit to bathe at least three times a week, in the summer and once a day in the winter. Kublai's Mongol courtiers soon copied this Chinese custom – which was probably just as well after wearing all those yak skins!

Grand canal

The Grand Canal in Peking reminded Marco of the canals in his hometown of Venice. It was built about 200 years before Mongol rule, but Kublai added to the city so that it extended to the Yangtze River. The canal was mostly used for transporting grain to the capital where the Great Khan had 58 granaries. Kublai's Chinese subjects provided the labour for all of his building projects as their duty.

'Marco was really impressed by the banknotes the people of China and the Mongols used,' said Rummage.

'Like that weird-looking Yuan note in the purse you bought from Youssef...' said Digby.

'Precisely. That note was specially made at Kublai's very own mint in Kanbalu,' declared Rummage, 'and anyone caught trying to forge, or make a copy of the Great Khan's banknotes, was executed.'

'Not worth the bother, then,' said Hester. 'So what were they made of?'

'Out of a kind of paper made from the the bark of mulberry trees,' Rummage went on.

'But what happened if they wore out or got ripped or something?' asked Digby.

'You just took them back to the royal mint and for a small payment you got brand-new ones,' chuckled Rummage.

 # Chinese treasures

Silkworms

For hundreds of years Chinese silk was highly valued in Europe, because no-one there knew how to make it. Europeans didn't know about the silkworm, and the Chinese were determined to keep it a secret. Silkworms were 'farmed' on mulberry tree farms, since they feed on mulberry leaves. The silk comes from the cocoons they spin, which are pounded to soften them before the silk is twisted into a fine thread. The Chinese make clothes, fans, parasols and kites out of silk.

WHEN MARCO POLO ARRIVED IN CHINA, TEA WAS A NATIONAL DRINK AND THE CHINESE WOULD HOLD TEA PARTIES IN THEIR FRAGRANT FLOWER GARDENS

Imperial Express

Probably because he travelled a lot, Marco became very impressed with Kublai Khan's post-house system. This was a kind of courier service, which used horsemen as well as runners. Marco says there were post-houses every 40 kiometres that were hotels fit for kings. Each stationmaster kept 400 horses in readiness. Couriers could cover about 500 km a day using the system. Each courier carried a small plaque with him on which was written where he had come from and in which direction he was going. Showing the plaque would make sure he travelled safely. Foot messengers came from villages spread five kilometres apart so no-one had to run more than that distance. They wore a belt with bells attached so the stationmaster could hear them coming and prepare the next runner to take over.

The Royal Mint

Kublai Khan made sure that every Chinese banknote was authenticated, or made real, in a special ceremony. Officers were specially appointed to sign their name and press their signet ring onto each note to make a mark. Then the notes were stamped in special colours. The paper money was circulated to all parts of the empire and could be exchanged for goods, or for gold or silver.

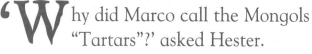

'Why did Marco call the Mongols "Tartars"?' asked Hester.

Rummage laughed. 'Because they were so warlike. In fact, people saw them as devils who commanded the armies of Hell. That's how much they were feared.'

'And misunderstood,' added Youssef.

'Yes,' said Rummage, 'but they were still brutal killers who showed no pity in battle, even if Marco did admire their fighting skills and bravery.'

'How come their armies were so good?' asked Digby.

'Speed, mostly,' replied Rummage. 'They were skilled horsemen. They even slept in the saddle while their horses grazed. And they were great shots with their bows and arrows. They could fire from the saddle, guiding their horses with their legs.'

'Wow!' exclaimed Digby.

'And when they were on the march,' added Youssef, 'they travelled light, living mostly on mare's milk. But if they had to move quickly and ran out of food, they lived off blood taken from veins in their horse's legs!'

'Ugh, that's horrid,' said the children, shuddering at the thought of it.

Mongolia

Mongolia, the homeland of the Mongols, has one of the harshest landscapes of any country on Earth. There are mountains and desert in the south, and vast windblown plains in the north. The Mongolians of today live very differently to their great ancestors. They are no longer warlike, but live simply, moving from place to place as they herd their flocks – just as their forebears did before the days of the Mongol Empire. They lead a hard life and practise many of the traditional tribal customs.

The Yurt

Often, the only sign of life on the bare plains is the round Mongol tent called a 'yurt'. The yurt is made of felt that comes from sheep's wool. The felt is laid over a frame of wooden poles that can be put up and taken down quickly so that the herdsmen can move on. The yurt, heated by animal dung, keeps its inhabitants very warm in the freezing Mongolian winter.

MONGOLIANS LOVE HORSES FOR THEIR SPIRIT, STRENGTH AND SURENESS OF FOOT, AND HERDSMEN SPEND MUCH OF THEIR LIVES IN THE SADDLE

'So how long was Marco Polo in China?' asked Digby.

'A long time,' said Rummage, 'almost 20 years. By that time, Kublai had grown so fond of the Polos that when they decided they'd like to leave in order to see their homeland again, Kublai didn't want to let them go.'

'That wasn't very fair, was it – after all Marco had done for him?' said Hester.

'You're right, Kublai had grown fond of Marco – but the emperor was getting old. I suppose he felt that Marco was part of his family now.'

'Did they escape?' asked Digby, his eyes lighting up.

'No, that would've been impossible – Kublai was too powerful. However, it just happened that they had a stroke of good luck. And just as well, too – because if Kublai had died, the Polos might not have been treated as well by whoever succeeded him to the throne.'

'So what happened?' asked Digby.

'It was Kublai's great nephew, named Il Khan, who started it,' said Youssef. 'He ruled Persia and wanted a young Mongol bride to rule beside him. Kublai was happy to send him one and the Polos, seeing a way out, persuaded the Great Khan that they should escort the bride-to-be.'

The Polos set sail

Royal junks

Kublai Khan gave the Polos a fleet of Chinese junks and enough food and equipment for the first part of their homeward journey. The name 'junk' comes from a Malaysian word that means 'boat'. Marco said they were huge, powerful vessels - with 60 cabins, compartments for storing goods and large enough to hold several smaller fishing boats.

China et Iava velis ex arundine   Schepen van China en Iava met rietten

JUNKS ARE MERCHANT SHIPS WITH A SINGLE DECK AND FOUR MASTS, EACH WITH A SQUARE SAIL

Goodbye Kublai

In January 1292, the Polos waved goodbye to Kublai Khan as their fleet of 14 junks with 600 crew set sail for the Persian Gulf. The journey was long and beset with problems. Of the original crew, only 18 survived, but Marco still managed to deliver the Mongol princess safely to her new husband. It was his last mission for the Great Khan.

Seafaring fables

In his travel diary, Marco wrote about the many wonders he encountered on his way home - although these were probably just fantastic fables he'd picked up from sailors whenever they put into port. He told of cannibals in Sumatra who drank milk from 'nuts as big as a human head' (coconuts), and made sugar and wine from palm trees. He wrote of the soldiers of Chipangu (Japan) who put gold and precious stones under their skin as a kind of body armour, and the monstrous 'roc' bird from Madagascar which was so strong it could lift three elephants.

Home at last

When Marco, his father and uncle arrived home they were dressed like Tartars. And to make matters worse, they had almost forgotten their own language. Marco's stories of the East were suspected of being just that – only stories. Because no-one had been there or had seen so many fabulous things before, it was hard to prove whether Marco was telling the truth. In fact, he was given the nickname 'Messer Millione' because of the stories he told of the Great Khan's millions – or perhaps because he told millions of stories...

Marco's stories

When he got home, Marco told stories about Kublai's war general Bayan-Hundred Eyes, whose name struck terror into the hearts of all who clashed with his fierce Mongol army. He described the battles he'd seen, like the earth-shaking one where a band of Mongol archers on horseback had bravely attacked an army of 60,000 warriors mounted on 2,000 trumpeting war elephants with huge tusks and wooden 'castles' on their backs. He recorded how 'The din and uproar was so great that God might have thundered and no man would have heard it!' And how Kublai Khan, from that time on, had always included elephants in his armies.

MARCO POLO DESCRIBED THE GREATNESS OF THE CHINESE CIVILISATION — ITS CITIES, ITS PEOPLE AND ITS WAY OF LIFE

'I bet the Polos were given a great "welcome home" party,' said Hester.

'Not at all,' said Rummage shaking his head sadly.

'That's awful,' said Digby, 'they should have rolled out the red carpet.'

'Actually, no-one knew who they were,' continued Rummage. 'And when the travellers tried to explain, the people of Venice just laughed at them. What they saw were three worn and weary travellers riding into the city wearing ragged, strange-looking clothes.'

'So they were dressed as Chinese people?' said Digby.

'Of course. They'd lived there for twenty years, don't forget,' said Rummage, 'and they didn't think they looked strange at all.'

'What did they do then?' asked Hester.

'Legend has it that the Polos invited the townspeople to a public banquet,' said Youssef. 'And when everyone had gathered round, they dramatically ripped open the linings of their ragged cloaks and out spilled a fortune in gems. The people gasped at this and also at the luxurious robes of satin and velvet the Polos were wearing underneath. There, for all to see, was the proof that they'd been to China, after all, and that it was a rich and exotic land.'

'I'd love to have seen the Venetians' faces,' grinned Hester.

'So would I,' laughed Youssef.

'I suppose he had to write down what he'd seen so people would believe him,' said Digby.

'Actually, he didn't write about his adventures until later,' said Rummage. 'In fact, he had to spend time in jail before the stories were scribbled down.'

'Jail!' exclaimed Hester. 'Surely he was a national hero!'

Rummage laughed. 'He wasn't put in a Venetian jail. But when Marco got home, war had started up again between the cities of Venice and Genoa. Each city was afraid of losing trade to the other. Marco was made a Gentleman Commander of a Venetian ship that was part of a fleet sent to fight the Genoese. Unfortunately, the Venetian fleet was destroyed and Marco's ship sunk. He, and thousands more, ended up in a Genoese jail.'

'So he whiled the time away by writing his book,' speculated Hester.

'Sort of…' continued Rummage. 'In jail he met a man called Rustichello, who came from Pisa. Rustichello used to retell old French romances. So, to pass the time, Marco dictated his tales to Rustichello, who wrote them down. Unfortunately, no original copy exists. Marco made a revised version himself, which was lost. The book we can read today is based on translations and translations of translations. So they're perhaps not as accurate as they could be.'

'So that's how we know all about Marco Polo,' said Digby. 'I think I'll buy that purse from you, Mr Rummage, if that's OK. You never know, it might bring me luck so that, one day, perhaps I'll dictate my adventures to someone.'

'It would make the smallest book in the world,' quipped Hester.

'Ah, but you never know what might happen in the future,' said Youssef. 'Digby might become a great traveller and explorer.'

'Telling lots of tall stories of his own, I suppose,' laughed Hester.

Fact or fiction

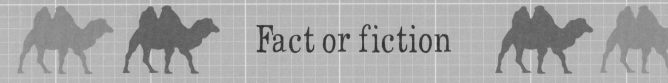

For many years after his death, Marco Polo's book was still considered a bit of a fairy tale. But it didn't take long before other people travelled to the East and it became clear that the places he'd talked about really did exist. However, there are some parts of Marco's story that we should take with a pinch of salt:

• Marco talked about Kublai Khan as though he were a chivalrous lord. He described his 10,000 falconers, 20,000 dog handlers and huge banquets with 40,000 guests. Probably, Marco exaggerated the figures to make Cathay and its ruler sound even grander than they were.

• The striped lions Marco talks about were probably tigers.

• Marco was never a military adviser to Kublai Khan. The battle he talks of happened before he got to China.

• There were no spirits of the desert, just wind and sand.

• The Japanese probably weren't cannibals.

In fact, some people believe Marco didn't go to China at all. Here are some reasons why:

• He didn't mention the Great Wall of China.

• He didn't talk about the Chinese tradition of foot binding, to keep women's feet small.

• The Polos aren't mentioned in any official Chinese record.

• Marco didn't mention tea-drinking, a Chinese tradition.

• Some of the places he describes are places he probably didn't go to.

• But as Marco himself said on his deathbed, when he was asked to admit his stories were false, 'I have not written half of those things which I saw.'